AF647109

DadA POETRY

an introduction

NIRALA SERIES

DADA POETRY

an introduction

William Seaton

Foreword by

Timothy Shipe

Curator, International Dada Archive

NIRALA

Nirala Publications
G.P.O. Box 7004
Daryaganj, New Delhi-110002
niralabooks@yahoo.co.in
www.niralapublications.com

First Edition 2013

ISBN-81-8250-035-4

Copyright@ William Seaton

Cover Design : S.A.A. Wasti

This book is sold subject to the condition that it shall not, by way of trade or otherwise, be lent, resold, hired out, or otherwise circulated without the publisher's prior written consent in any form of binding or cover other than that in which it is p ublished and without a similar condition including this condition being imposed on the susequent purchaser and without limiting the rights under copyright reserved, no part of this publication may be reproduced, stored in or introduced into a retrieval system or transmitted in any form or by any means (electronic, mechanical, photocopying, recording or otherwise) without prior written permission of the above mentioned publisher of this book.

Printed at
H.S. Offset Printers
New Delhi-110002

Foreword

Thirty years of engagement with the bibliography of Dada have provided me with many occasions to lament the relative neglect of German Dada poetry in the English-speaking world. It is true that Rex W. Last's critical survey *German Dadaist Literature* (New York: Twayne, 1973) gave relatively early attention to three of the poets of German Dada (Schwitters, Ball, and Arp), and that in the ensuing decades monographs have appeared in English on these writers and others. But translators have paid scant attention to the poetic output of the German-speaking participants in the Dada movement. Contrast this with the prolific activity of English translators of the Francophone Dada poets, especially Breton, Tzara, and, indeed, Arp; why, after thirty-six years, has there never been a *Collected German Writings* to supplement Joachim Neugroschl's version of Arp's *Collected French Writings* (London: Calder and Boyars, 1974)?

So here, at last, is William Seaton's anthology of four German Dada poets. Of the four poets represented in this collection, only Arp has been extensively translated into English (and then chiefly from the French—see above). All four are included in Willard Bohn's anthology *The Dada Market* (Carbondale: Southern Illinois University Press, 1993), but with only two poems apiece. A determined search will uncover other translations scattered in literary magazines and anthologies. But here, for the first time, the English-speaking reader will find a generous sampling of German Dada poetry in a single volume.

The emphasis here is, clearly, Zurich Dada. The poets presented were all participants in the Cabaret Voltaire and in the initial phase of what grew into an international movement. This provides a thematic unity to the volume that might have been difficult to achieve had the translator attempted to encompass the Dada poetry of Berlin, Cologne, and Hanover as well as Zurich. The choice of Hennings, Huelsenbeck, Arp, and Ball immerses us in a particular place and time: neutral Zurich at the height of the Great War. Of these poets, only Ball and Hennings remained in Swiss exile after the end of the war (following a few brief forays back to their native Germany), but there is something poignant in the fact that all four of them would eventually die in Switzerland: Arp in Basel, the other three in Ticino within a five-mile radius.

So, here are twenty-two Dada poems, twenty-one translated from German along with one requiring no translation, written, for the most part, in one multilingual country, published in another multilingual country, presented in the hope that the Anglophone reader will be tantalized and encouraged to seek out more of the literary fruits of Dada.

—**Timothy Shipe**
Curator, International Dada Archive
University of Iowa Libraries

Acknowledgements

The Huelsenbeck poems "Marfarka," "Death," "End of the World, "To Ludwig the Flirt" first appeared in *Adirondack Review,* vol. X, no. 2 (winter 2009).

Emmy Hennings' "Ether Stanzas" and Hugo Ball's "The Dance of Death" first appeared in the fall 2008 *Read and Destroy.*

"A Note on Emmy Hennings," Twilight Song," "After the Cabaret," first appeared in *Maintenant 4.*

Huelsenbeck's "Tree" and "Streams," and Arp's "Roses Stroll the Streets of Porcelain," as well as a version of "The Swallow Testicle" using the title "Kasper's Dead" appeared in *Mad Blood #3* (June 2004).

Earlier versions of Huelsenbeck's "Tree," Streams, and "Schalaben- Schalabai Schalamezomai" appeared in *Chelsea 59* (1995).

Some of the essay "Sweet Treason" was delivered at the World Poetry Café in Saugerties New York July 13, 2007.

Contents

DADA POETRY

an introduction

An Introduction to Dada

I. Dada

To begin with I shall attempt to compensate for the restless instability of my subject by containing my remarks within the bounds of a conventional essay, intending to present with some measure of order, lucidity, and logic an elusive, exasperating movement that defies classification and discussion, flies in the face of rationality, and thumbs its nose not just at received wisdom and sacred cows, but, indeed, at all our normal habits of thought. Rather like the blows and koans of Rinzai Zen and the cunning dreams we all conjure nightly, the purest manifestations of Dada seek to shake the observer into enlightenment through oblique attacks, saucing the onslaught with wit, political passion, and effervescent bohemianism. This exposition will, quite properly, be succeeded by examples of Dada poetry which will invoke the "ghost voices" of these old poets. We will test in this volume whether their spells remain efficacious for readers in the twenty-first century.

Since water-drinking poets sparred with wine's party in the ancient world, culture has always spawned counter-culture, and Harold Bloom has recently taught us to see literary history as a series of Oedipal displacements. But since the Industrial Revolution and the Romantic movement, artists have been feeling particularly adversarial. The late Victorian period brought explosive economic growth, but also fearsome class conflict involving not just labor organization, but also anarchist violence. The age boasted a magisterial academy, but also self-conscious outsiders, independents, secessionists, symbolists, decadents, expressionists, futurists, cubists, and countless other schools of more or less oppositional artistic practice. For these artists condemnation by mainstream critics and galleries could be a point of pride.

As World War I raged, transgression was approaching the norm in aesthetic circles, and a pose of total revolt emerged which, despite such precursors as Rimbaud, Lautréamont, and Jarry, was new in its absoluteness, its self-conscious *esprit,* and, above all, its collective character. Artists rejected not merely the older generation's art, but conventional politics, morality, the entire "straight" lifestyle, to use more contemporary jargon.[1] In Zurich, Switzerland, a group of artists, most of them draft-dodgers, disillusioned veterans, and far-left revolutionaries, with a variety of national origins and languages, sought to construct a liberated zone in the Café Voltaire where Hugo Ball (a deserter) and Emmy Hennings (a singer and *diseuse,* or, as one might say, spoken word performer) had opened a cabaret.

According to poet Richard Huelsenbeck:

> The Balls came to Zurich without a cent and left their fate to chance. They had nothing to eat and sat on the shores of Lake Zurich, envying the well-fed swans for their feed. Since Ball did not have a valid passport, he was arrested by the police but released after a short time. All his efforts at finding a job and earning money were to no avail. Ball had taken it into his head to be a waiter since he owned a black

> suit and a white shirt. But, one day, while sitting with Emmy on a bench at the lake, he suddenly became hysterical, and just as he was about to throw the package containing the suit into the water, it burst open. The suit and the shirt fell into the clay and the sand. This accident spelled the end of his dream of being a waiter . . . Emmy went to Niedendorf, the oldest part of town, and entered one of the many seedy music halls to talk to the owner about selling the suit to a waiter or a performer. Instead, she was asked whether she sang. The interview ended with her being hired. Ball was to be her pianist, and so the period of famine was over.
>
> (Dada Drummer 4-5)

Before long Ball and Hennings were programming events for an artists' cabaret, and the entertainment became unpredictable and radically innovative: "I recited my new 'authentic' Negro poems, and the audience thought they were wonderful . . . Hugo was sitting at the piano, playing classical music, Brahms and Bach. Then he switched over to dance music. The drunken students pushed their chairs aside and began spinning around. There were almost no women in the cabaret. It was too wild, too smoky, too way out. Hugo had written a poem against war and murderous insanity. Emmy recited it, Hugo accompanied her on the piano, and the audience chimed in, with a growl, murdering the poem." (Dada Drummer 9)

The spirit, if not the precise events, of a Café Voltaire evening is recorded in Janco's painting, here described by Arp:

> "On a platform in an overcrowded room, splotched with color, are seated several fantastic characters . . . Tzara, Ball, Huelsenbeck, Madame Hennings, and your humble servant. We are putting on one of our big Sabbaths. The people around us are shouting, laughing, gesticulating. We reply with sighs of love, salvos of hiccups, poems, and the bow-wows and meows of medieval bruitists. Tzara makes his bottom jump like the belly of an oriental dancer. Janco plays on an invisible violin and bows down to the ground. Madame Hennings with a face like a madonna attempts a split. Huelsenbeck keeps pounding on a big drum, while Ball, pale as a plaster dummy, accompanies him on the piano."
>
> (Motherwell xx)

Some evenings may have struck an accidental visitor as chaotic, but in retrospect the critic can discern virtually the entire repertory of modernist technique: first of all abstraction (which to some at the first seemed the party slogan of Dada), fragmentation, collage, performance art, conceptual art, aleatory work, simultaneity, sound poems *(bruitisme* or *Klangdichtung), objets trouvés,* interest in ethnological "primitive" culture material and popular culture, even pranks, such as sending false news items to newpapers. (See Motherwell 131.)

Like such traditional artists as Tibetan and Navajo sand painters, Dadaists foregrounded the evanescence and insubstantiality of their work and of the perceptual flow that provides the raw materials of which all artifacts are made. According to Huelsenbeck,

> Simultaneity is against what has become, and for what is becoming . . . While I, for example, become successively aware that I boxed an old woman on the ear yesterday and washed my hands an hour ago, the screeching of a streetcar brake and the crash of a brick falling off the roof next door reach my ear simultaneously and my (outward or inward) eye

> rouses itself to seize, in the simultaneity of these events, a swift meaning of life.
>
> (Motherwell 35-36).

Artists have often found pleasure in imagining immortality for their constructed art objects. Yet Breton, a few years into the trajectory established by Dada, so embraced the ephemeral as to declare: "It is inadmissible that a man should leave any trace of his passage on earth." (Motherwell 203) Ginsberg's fondness for snapshots and, in poetry, "first thought best thought" seems classical by contrast.

The subjective experience is well suggested by Tristan Tzara:

> Gala night – simultaneous poem 3 languages, protest noise Negro music/ Hosenlatz [trouser-fly] Ho osenlatz/piano Typerrary Lanterna magica demonstration last proclamation!! Invention dialogue!! DADA! latest novelty!!! Bourgeois syncope, BRUITIST music, latest rage, song Tzara dance protests – the big drum – red light, policemen – songs cubist paintings post cards song Cabaret Voltaire – patented simultaneous poem Tzara Ho osenlatz and van Hoddis Hü ülsenbeck Hoosenlatz whirlwind Arp-

two-step demands liquor smoke toward the bells/a whispering of: arrogance/silence Mme Hennings, Janco declaration, transatlantic art = the people rejoice star hurled upon the cubist tinkle dance (Motherwell 235-6).

Another event:

(Music, dances, theories, manifestoes, poems, paintings, costumes, masks)

In the presence of a compact crowd Tzara demonstrates, we demand we demand the right to piss in different colors, Huelsenbeck demonstrates, Ball demonstrates, Arp "Erklärung" (Statement), Janco "meine Bilder" (my pictures), Heusser "eigene Kompositionen" (original compositions) the dogs bay and the dissection of Panama on the piano on the piano and dock – shouted Poem – shouting and fighting in the hall, first row approves second row declares itself incompetent the rest shout, who is the strongest, the big drum is brought in, Huelsenbeck against 200. Ho osenlatz accentuated by the very big drum and little bells on his left foot – the people protest shout smash windowpanes kill each other demolish fight here come the police interruption.

Boxing resumed: Cubist dance, costumes by Janco, each man his own big drum on his head, noise, Negro music / trabatgea bonoooooo oo ooooo / 5 literary experiments: Tzara in tails stands before the curtain, stone sober for the

> animals, and explains the new aesthetic: gymnastic poem, concert of vowels, bruitist poem, static poem chemical arrangement of ideas, "Biriboom, biriboom" saust der Ochs im Kreis herum (the ox dashes around in a ring) (Huelsenbeck), vowel poems a a ò, I e o, a i ï, new interpretation the subjective folly of the arteries the dance of the heart on burning buildings and acrobatics in the audience. More outcries, the big drum, piano and impotent cannon, cardboard costumes torn off the audience hurls itself into puerperal fever interrupt. The newspapers dissatisfied simultaneous poem for 4 voices + simultaneous work for 300 hopeless idiots.
>
> (Motherwell 236-7)

Norm violation is central to many definitions of Dada: Breton declared that "Dada is artistic free thinking (Motherwell 203)." (Motherwell 37) For Schwitters, Merz, his own individual strain of Dada, "stands for freedom from all fetters." (Motherwell 59) But this destructive, skeptical turn of mind was equally merciless to Dada itself. Tzara could make Dada theory simple as pie: "DADA DOES NOT MEAN ANYTHING" ("Dada Manifesto 1918" Tzara 4). Or, as

Picabia put it, "Dada smells of nothing, it is nothing, nothing, nothing" (Motherwell 37). But nirvana also means nothing, extinction, "blowing out," and that void Hindus call sunyatta[2] yawns only in the last instance, the most piercing glance into the heart of things. One move short of the ultimate there is a great apocalyptic clearing of the throat: "We are like a raging wind that rips up the clothes of clouds and prayers, we are preparing the great spectacle of disaster, conflagration and decomposition. Preparing to put an end to mourning, and to replace tears by sirens spreading from one continent to another. Clarions of intense joy, bereft of that poisonous sadness" (Tzara 8). Here dualism explodes, as it does in Buddhist philosophy. "Order = disorder; ego = non-ego; affirmation = negation" (Tzara 7). By way of instruction and illustration art must be turned inside out to produce anti-art. Nonsense comes on deadly serious, while all the grave matters go about in motley.

The Dada rejection of dualism by no means implies aloofness from worldly affairs. Dadaists, having ridden the bull of truth in action, returned to the world.[33]

The movement, which was born out of revulsion to WWI, questioned the social order no less rigorously than the established philosophical and artistic assumptions. In a Europe in which a surging socialist movement (including vigorous far-left and anarchist factions) coexisted with the decaying remnants of European feudalism, many of the Dadaists were political revolutionaries, and not a few, after antinomian, sometimes libertine youth, went on to disciplined Communist Party membership. Huelsenbeck himself declared that "Dada is German Bolshevism" (Motherwell 44). The photocollagist John Heartfield (who had changed his name from Helmut Herzfelde as an act of protest against German militarism) produced powerful propaganda posters first for socialism and then specifically targeted against the Nazi regime. Whether the Dadaists really controlled the Ministry of Culture in the short-lived revolutionary regime of 1919 (during the same ferment that led to the murders of Spartacists Rosa Luxemburg and Karl Liebknecht), there is no question about their extraordinary program which demanded:

> 1. The international revolutionary union of all creative and intellectual men and women on the basis of radical communism;
>
> 2. The introduction of progressive unemployment through comprehensive mechanization of every field of activity. Only by unemployment does it become possible for the individual to achieve certainty as to the truth of life and finally become accustomed to experience;
>
> 3. The immediate expropriation of property (socialization) and the communal feeding of all; further, the erection of cities of light, and gardens which will belong to society as a whole and prepare man for a state of freedom.
>
> (Motherwell 41-2)

The program proceeds through such benevolent measures as free meals "for all creative and intellectual men and women," and "150 circuses for the enlightenment of the proletariat," but also strangely satiric measures aping totalitarianism: "Compulsory adherence of all clergymen and teachers to the dadaist articles of faith," "the simultaneist poem as a Communist state prayer," "submission of all laws and decrees to the Dadaist central council for approval," and, finally, "Immediate regulation of all sexual relations according to the views of international Dadaism through establishment of a Dadaist sexual center." Patently, the agenda is not designed to please a politician of any school other than that of the imagination.[4]

More superficial perhaps, though tonic nonetheless, is the assertive bohemianism of the Dada crew. The distinctive twentieth century concept of the "hip"[5] vision generated art which asserted its privileged origins in a knowing coterie who see through the lies and myths that con the square. The central claim of hipness is that one is hip to some jive, to political shucking, élite artistic signifying, and pulpit hypocrisy. The hip produce art whose very birth is midwived by resistance and rebellion. This can sound rather arrogant: Picabia addresses the public "What are you doing here, plunked down like serious oysters . . . I'll just go on telling you all fools (Motherwell 37)." Allied to this claim that the hip know more, that they see what the straight world cannot are such related twentieth century brands of irony as camp and kitsch on the one hand, or the insider mystique of jargon, whether that of the inner city streets or of the post-structuralist academy. A similar model is apparent in the twentieth century discourse of "double-consciousness" (in DuBois'sense) through which African-Americans categorized as "other" gain vatic authority to compensate for their suffering material disadvantage.

All of these are, again, "doubled" ways of seeing, in which one view is privileged for truth or taste in spite of the other's domination in good society. In a similar way

Buddhism abounds in stories of the enlightened who appear frivolous or mad, just as Dada had to many. Here the rejection of the norm, the "alternative" character of the new insight and the new art is the guarantee of its authenticity and value. If that is the theoretical goal, how, in practical terms, does one split culture like a walnut and produce self-reflective "hip" art?

Methods vary: simple travesties of received ideas, a quest for truth in forbidden drugs, the technical incompetent playing that, for early punk, meant "unprofessional" and, thus, uncommodified. The dadaists developed a rich repertory. This is Ball's account of the birth of sound poetry:

> "I invented a new species of verse, 'verse without words,' or sound poems, in which the balancing of the vowels is gauged and distributed only to the value of the initial line. The first of these I recited tonight [1915]. I had a special costume designed for it. My legs were covered with a cothurnus of luminous blue cardboard, which reached up to my hips so that I looked like an obelisk"
>
> (in *Motherwell*, xix).

The setting and costume guarantee a show, while the abstract flow of sound, whatever its charms, must retreat from signification, and leave the listener questioning poetry itself.

Sometimes the impact of Dada performance art was more widely disseminated when staging occurred outside the gallery or cabaret with its voluntary audience. Johannes Baader[6] liked to call himself Oberdada, or, in spells of somewhat grander exaltation "president of world justice," and "secret president of the League of Superdadaist Intertelluric Nations," and "president of the terrestrial globe in the saddle of Dada." Baader inspired the situationists and other guerrilla performers with such acts as his denunciation of the Weimar Republic from its visitors' gallery. In the name of the Central Dada Council of the World Revolution he rained leaflets down upon the heads of liberal and reactionary legislators alike. On another occasion he entered the Berlin Cathedral just as the sermon was beginning. In a commanding voice, Baader addressed the worshippers: "Wait a moment! Let me ask you, what is Jesus Christ after all? He is a sausagehead!" [7] (Others, it must be added, later recalled his delivering a homily in which he maintained that Dadaism would save the world.) Judged to be mentally ill, Baader was released from custody. No one ever saw a copy of his newspaper *The Green Corpse*. (Motherwell, 149) His great wish was to construct a monument to humanity in the form of an enormous pyramid.

The stories are numerous, tempting, and, in the case of Dada, unlike most other art, highly relevant. In the case of such narratives as the invention of the name Dada the retelling, the misprision, the willful distortion seems often to constitute the art. But the time has arrived for texts. These poems, though frozen in their present concrete form and lacking the spontaneity, the unpredictability the Dadaists so prized, can, I believe, still disturb, and they can still enlighten. At first acquaintance they may charm with their ebullience or their sweet malaise. They may also move the reader with their righteous passionate protest. The possibilities of art are interrogated to the extent that it is ambiguous at last whether they are multiplied marvelously or wholly collapsed. The poems, at their best, are like the man in the Lotus Sutra, crying out in agitation, seeking to save his family from the flames. And we suddenly know, even if only for a moment, that all the order in our lives, whether political, aesthetic, or cosmic is, in the words another Buddhist text, the Diamond Sutra, "as a fault of vision . . . a mock show, dew drops, or a bubble, a dream, a lightning flash, or cloud." And to compensate for that vast incertitude, is the knowledge that just as all things have Buddha-nature, Dada is everywhere. As a Dada once said, "People are all angels and live in the sky."

References

Huelsenbeck, Richard. Memoirs of a Dada Drummer. Ed. Hans J. Kleinschmidt. Foreword by Rudolf E. Kuenzli. Berkeley: University of California, 1991.

Robert Motherwell (editor). The Dada Painters and Poets. Cambridge (Mass.): Harvard, 1981

Notes

1 Following WWI the general revulsion against war was expressed in such phenomena as the Kellogg-Briand Pact, the Oxford Pledge, and the League of Nations . The artists were in advance of the public as well as more intense and flamboyant in their antiwar stance. The parallel with the Vietnam era in the USA is irresistible.

2 Similarly, according to Ko Won, for the Japanese Dadaist and Buddhist Takahashi Shinkichi dada expressed perfectly "the Buddhist doctrine of anatman. . . or no-self, no-soul, which professes that all things, including self, are without permanence, constantly in change, and there is no separate self, whether as body or soul, sense or consciousness. In the Buddhist view, everything is in fact selfless, mere illusion, and therefore the whole world is empty" (35 *Buddhist Elements in Dada*. New York: NYU Univ. Press, 1977). In his view dada and Buddhism are linked by "the notion of nothingness, the dis-

credit of words and logic, and anticonventionalism (11-12).

3 I refer to the famous Bull or Ox-Herding pictures that illustrate the path to enlightenment. The terms here are from the version in Paul Reps, *Zen Flesh, Zen Bones.* Garden City NY : Doubleday, 1961.

4 Of course, one of the most celebrated slogans of Paris in '68 was *"L'imagination au pouvoir!"* See Walter Lewino's book of the same title (Paris: Losfeld, 1968) for other graffiti from the period.

5 According to J. L. Dillard the term derives from the Wolof hipicat, meaning "man who is aware or has his eyes open." (p. 119, *Black English.* New York, Random House, 1972). Noted here, though irrelevant, is the meaning for hip in the OED: "chronic depression, the "blues." In this case the word was short for hypochondria.

6 I am disappointed to report that Baader seems to have no connection with the Red Army Faction, called the Baader-Meinhof Gang, active in Germany during the era of the Weather Underground. Baader-Meinhof is currently enjoying a vogue marked by books, movies, and commemorative t-shirts.

7 Is the story more flavorful in German? *"Am 17.11.1918 unterbricht Baader einen im Berliner Dom gehaltenen Gottesdienst. Raoul Hausmann schildert den Vorfall so: "Als der Hofprediger Dryander seine Predigt beginnen wollte, rief Baader mit lauter Stimme: Einen Augenblick! Ich frage sie, was ist Ihnen Jesus Christus? Er ist Ihnen Wurst ...! Weiter kam er nicht; es gab einen fürchterlichen Tumult, Baader wurde verhaftet und eine Anklage gegen ihn erhoben. Infolge "krankhafter Störung der Geistestätigkeit" (sodas Berliner Landgericht) wird das Verfahren gegen ihn eingestellt."*

Sweet Treason:
On Literary Translation

Literary translation is clearly altogether different from the translation of technical writing of any other form of information-oriented discourse. If one translates an article to appear in a journal of experimental physics, the goal is to convey the data as clearly as possible. Such texts as a car repair manual, a newspaper, or, indeed, a lecture on translation may be rendered into another language without any loss of meaning whatsoever.

In fact, some translations of poetry are almost as straightforward. Unpretentious interlinear translations of Greek and Latin poetry were once popular with students as cribs. The translator who primarily seeks to facilitate the reader's access to the original is engaged in a pedagogical exercise, providing, perhaps, a literal prose translation along with annotations. Even in this case, however, the translator cannot avoid semantic decisions with which others might differ.

At the other end of the spectrum are translations read for their own literary value and judged by the same standards as other poetry. Sometimes such a translator seeks to devise cross-cultural analogies (such as saying "god" for "Zeus" or substituting English iambs for Greek dactyls). A poet/translator may aim to assert the spirit of the original in a holistic way, but, having abandoned literal fidelity, any license may be justified. Such versions may slide entirely from the category of translations to become *hommages* or poems "inspired by" other texts.

The problems of translation go far beyond even the connotations of words and the recognition of irony and intertextual allusion. A distinguishing characteristic of the aesthetic text, of literature as opposed to other forms of discourse, is that form is content. Therefore the translator must consider prosody, rhyme, vocalic clusters, rhythm, alliteration, level of diction, and countless other elements, all of which are operative or significant in varying degrees in a given poem.

The upshot is that poetry has been called flat-out untranslatable by definition.[1] My title is derived from the saying *"traduttore, traditore"*. A French version, laced with misogyny, suggests that a translation's fidelity to the original is inversely proportional to its aesthetic value: *"Les traductions sont comme les femmes, ou belles ou fidèles."* Unfortunately, though, the less beautiful are not always the more faithful, nor are loveliest always least faithful.

The translator pursuing a goal of word-for-word correspondence will rapidly discover that content can be preserved only at the cost of form, and retaining formal elements often means sacrificing a share of literal meaning. And where are grace and charm by then? Even a commitment to some semblance of original form does not end the difficulties. Should the translator of *Beowulf* who rejects free verse seek to retain the four beat accentual meter (not to mention the alliteration, the caesurae, and the kennings) to give a stronger flavor of Old English?[2] Or should he render the text in iambic pentameter, as the typical epic meter of English? Perhaps heroic couplets would reflect the more highly patterned conventions of the original, though rhyme plays virtually no part in Old English prosody. In some cases the patterning cannot possibly be reproduced. The quantitative measures of Greek, Latin, and Arabic poetry, for instance, are virtually impossible to duplicate in English.[3] In a non-tonal language the translator cannot even try to imitate the tonal patterns used in poetic convention in Chinese and in Yoruba. Opposite responses to decisions about formal convention are the chief difference between nineteenth century translations and those of today.

The brilliantly original stylist Vladimir Nabokov places himself among the advocates of literal translation.

"There is a certain small Malayan bird of the thrush family which is said to sing only when tormented in an unspeakable way by a specially trained child at the annual Feast of

Flowers. There is Casanova making love to a harlot while looking from the window at the nameless tortures inflicted on Damiens. These are the visions that sicken me when I read the "poetical" translations from martyred Russian poets by some of my famous contemporaries. A tortured author and a deceived reader, this is the inevitable outcome of arty paraphrase. The only object and·justification of translation is the conveying of the most exact information possible and this can be only achieved by a literal translation, with notes."[4]

Nabokov may be been replying to the challenge in the preface to Robert Lowell's very successful 1962 collection *Imitations*:

> "Strict metrical translators still exist. They seem to live in a pure world untouched by contemporary poetry. Their difficulties are bold and honest, but they are taxidermists, not poets, and their poems are likely to be stuffed birds."[5]

Instead Lowell took every freedom: "I have dropped lines, moved lines, moved stanzas, changes images and altered meter and intent." More than one twentieth century translation has been made by a writer who knew little or none of the original language.

Most translators operate somewhere between these extremes. One who seeks to bring as much of the original into another language as possible will use the prosodic and thematic decisions already made by the author, whereas the advocate of free-wheeling taste-governed approach will aim primarily to create a compelling text in English, but most translators fall somewhere between and are thus confronted with a myriad decisions governed by the competing claims of accuracy and art. A sensitive writer might hesitate between highly dissimilar choices.

> Translation is the art of revelation. It makes the unknown known. The translator artist has the fever and craft to recognize, re-create, and reveal the work of the other artist. But even when famous at home, the work comes into an alien city as an orphan with no past to its readers. In rags,

> hand-me-downs, or dramatic black capes of glory, it is surprise, morning, a distinctive stranger. The orphan is Don Quijote de la Mancha in Chicago.[6]

And Barnstone's compelling images remind us of the value of translation. Just as all human culture is profoundly collective, and technological innovations spread rapidly even in antiquity,[7] poetry, a form of verbal technology, is continually refreshed and renewed by innovation which may arise with the excuse of a foreign text as well as though the ingenuity of a native. Roman translators of Greek work like Ennius, Naevius, and Livius Andronicus presented the Romans with models, just as the Korean, Vietnamese, and Japanese scholars adopted Chinese conventions. Catullus translated Sappho and popularized her meter in Latin. Xuan Zang brought Buddhist scriptures to China from India just as today missionaries translate the Bible for the remotest tribes. John Gower wrote in English, Latin, and French around the same time that Chaucer adopted the continental habit of rhyming (as well as translating *Romance of the Rose* and Boethius), and in the next century Wyatt and Surrey learned from Italy to write sonnets. Translation of newly available ancient works, and, in particular, the Greek classics, was a constituent part of the Renaissance. Then, as Pound has pointed out, the Elizabethan age was a great age of translation, producing Chapman's version of Homer, Golding's of Ovid, Gavin Douglas' and Surrey's Vergil. In the early twentieth century the Imagist movement imitated Chinese poetry.[8] Poets such as Pound, Rexroth, Bly, Gary Snyder and Paul Blackburn have made translation a significant portion of their oeuvre. Translated works such as the morality play *Everyman* or Fitzgerald's *Rubaiyat* are treated very nearly as original works, while some translations (such as the King James Bible, A. W. Schlegel's Shakespeare or Baudelaire's Poe) are regarded as classics.

The pitfalls and peaks of translation illustrate, as though through a microscope, problematics inherent in all communication. Few of us feel we have access to absolute Truth; rather, we are conscious of constantly managing with what data we can pick up. Further, every speaker, whether lecturing from a podium or sharing a pillow with a single auditor, is conscious that words do not quite adequately bear meaning. Scarcely able to know our own minds, we formulate utterances by makeshift and jerry-rigging. We have all known of cases in which a listener understands in a way that differs widely from that consciously intended by the speaker, or in which two auditors have altogether different interpretations while the speaker's mind remains unknown. Even the simplest of conversational conventions may be laden with potential oblique signification. A simple "good morning" may carry tones of flirtation, censure, concern, etc. How much more mysterious are words of love, of philosophy, or of art! The notorious vogue of deconstruction taught us, at least, that every utterance is inaccurate, that our writings persist only "under erasure".[9] The forked tongue in its figurative sense is part of what makes us human. The flawed material that does make it to the page will be incompletely and inaccurately understood by readers in an ever-metamorphosing variety of readings.

Thus, the problems of translation are simply a particular category of the problems of communication in general. The Greek rhetorician Gorgias taught the most uncompromising skepticism,[10] declaring three remarkable propositions:

1. Nothing exists.
2. Even if something were to exist, nothing could be known about it.
3. Even if something could be known, it could not be communicated.

Gorgias, of course, ignored these limitations to become a celebrated man of words, composing works that were described as magical and incantatory, with an effect that, according to the author, could only be compared to taking drugs.

Most thinkers would not follow Gorgias (or even take him seriously), but few would dispute that the formulations of language are never perfectly efficient, that further information is inevitably lost upon reception, and that aesthetic texts are dramatically more imperfect, because more ambitious, than other kinds of writing. Even the greatest poetic composition falls short of a complete record of vision and it is always imperfectly understood by the consumer. But we no sooner stop singing for this reason than we stop declaring love to our lovers (or our gods) because language seems not quite up to the task. We tell lies and truths and monstrous combinations of the two to our fellow humans daily, and we while away some of our time under the sun telling tales to beguile the day, singing a song of joy over a full belly, and later making love with words in the dark.

In the first instance, these particular poems are worth translation because they are good poems. In other words, most peoples' consumption of them has proven productive: things happen, ideas spark, a laugh or shudder rises, or a sudden pleasure. In recent years, I have performed these versions many times before live audiences and have found that they retain their charm. In theme, they record a peculiarly uncompromising vision of the desolation of the modern world, though the trickster spirit in the background is generally piping a jester's tune. In form, too, they clearly established parameters for the avant-garde for the last hundred years.

Of course, perfect literary translation is altogether impossible. Despite its value in refreshing the word, keeping possibilities open, and protecting literature from parochialism, literary translation is often accorded little respect by poets (who consider it unoriginal) or by scholars (who see it as lacking the rigor of research and, in any event, never meant for specialists). Often thankless, the task would be terminally frustrating were it not for the fact that translation can provide the most unexpected rewards.

Hennings' poems, from shortly before the dada period, are metered and rhymed, representing in a way the last expiring sweetness of German Romanticism, by now just a bit decayed. Or the reader may prefer to hear in her stanzas some hint of her melodious singing voice. I have striven to respect her forms, though I did not always preserve them exactly.

Huelsenbeck and Arp used free verse for the most part. (The marvelous parody of *Minnesang* "DADA-Schalmai" is a notable exception.) Without having to chase after rhymes and metrical feet, the translator is able to approach the considerable problems in language, tone, and sometimes even syntax. Context provides little clue when working with the texts of such radical innovators whose intention was more often to overturn readers' expectations than to fulfill them.

Even when misunderstood, foreign texts can be enlightening. And then it sometimes happens, and it might be just when one is concentrating on cutting one's losses, that another's vision seems fixed precisely in mid-leap, a memorable felicity will bloom, and a poem that is a poem regardless of being a translation, emerges.

All communication (including reading and translating) is a search for meaning. There can be no perfect translation, just as there is no flawless man, no poem to end all poems, but that is no reason to stop talking, and singing, and translating.

Notes

[1] These words are from Roman Jakobson's paper "On Linguistic Aspects of Translation."

[2] This is the strategy, for instance, of E. R. Eddison's *Egil's Saga*. He complains of the only earlier translation's "flaccid paraphrase" and "Latinized constructions."

[3] Though Arabic, for instance, also uses true quantitative verse. Noble attempts have been made by enthusiastic classically trained poets such as Swinburne to write quantitative verse in English, but the fact is that the duration of vowels are not audible to most English

speakers.

[4] Vladimir Nabokov, *Strong Opinions.*

[5] Perhaps Nabokov, with his enormous collections of Lepidoptera, took this last insult personally. To some taxidermy is an art.

[6] Willis Barnstone, *The Art of Translation.*

[7] Authorities seem to feel that alphabetic writing was invented once only, though Meso-America and perhaps China developed other systems.

[8] This is not invariably a gain. In modern times, translation has served the dubious function of smoothing regional differences and bringing second-hand surrealism, for instance, to dozens of countries almost simultaneously, interrupting whatever had been developing locally.

[9] The term often appears in Derrida's *Of Grammatology.* This is particularly true of poetic texts whose especial province is the ambiguous, the ambivalent, the conflicted, and the mysterious.

[10] In his philosophical work *On Nature or the Non-Existent,* which some readers take to be

a parodic response to Parmenides. Those curious about this fascinating figure may see my essay "Gorgias of Leontini," in the *Ancient Greek Authors* volume (176) of the Dictionary of Literary Biography series, edited by Ward W. Briggs, Jr.

Dada Poetry

One

Emmy Hennings

I begin with Emmy Hennings whose poetry is richly suffused with a tone that goes far to explain the origins of dada. She establishes a mood that was to persist in German art, particularly theater and painting, for decades. In her poems a malaise, a conviction of some intolerable derangement in things is linked with a nearly desperate eroticism, yet expressed with redemptive poise and precision.

Emmy Hennings met Hugo Ball, whom she later married, at the Cabaret Simplizissimus in Munich where she was performing in 1913. She had already published a number of poems in avant-garde and leftist journals as well as having cultivated her skills as a performance and cabaret artist. Though much of her work was ephemeral songs, dances, and recitations of which we have only the barest record, she also published a volume of poetry entitled *Die Letzte Freude* in which some of the following texts first appeared.

As a performer she engaged in dada acts of provocation, but also acted (in the German premiere of Andreev's *The Life of a Man,* for instance), danced, sang, and presented puppet shows. She was called "the shining star of the Voltaire" in the *Zuricher Post* and Ball always said she was a fully responsible collaborator. After the Café Voltaire closed, she and Ball worked together under the name Arabella, appearing in hotels and restaurants.

She took risks, agitating for revolution and forging documents for draft dodgers (for which she received a brief prison sentence). She worked for a time as a prostitute and her one surviving child was brought up by her mother.

Her work expresses the malaise of the era and the Bohemian reaction, heavy with dread yet scintillating with spirit and extravagance. The "Twilight Song" with its ambiguous ending, critiques Wagner while expressing the horror and, to use a more contemporary term, "belatedness" of the twentieth century. Many of her lyrics seem in a way the counterpoint to George Grosz's scenes of bestial carnality among the ruling class. With the world disintegrating, she, too grasps after some version of love. Neither her memoir of dada *Das Brandmal: Ein Tagebuch* nor her autobiography *Ruf und Echo* has been translated into English.

In a statement rich with historical ironies, Johannes Becher, the Expressionist and

Spartacist who later became a Stalinist apparatchik and repressed the same radical artists and intellectuals whose milieu had once been his own, wrote "It was in Munich, at the Café Stefanie, where I recited for you, Emmy, poems that I dared tell only you."

Twilight Song

for Hugo Ball

Octaves reel, and through the grey years — echoes
as heaps of days collapse upon themselves.
I want only to be yours.
Within my tomb my blond hair grows;
in elderberry bushes live strange folk.
A pale curtain whispers "homicide."
Two eyes range restless through the room,
inside our cupboards spirits hide.
Little fir trees are the children's souls
and ancient oaks the souls of aged men
that whisper of miscarried lives.
The cliff-king sings an old, old tune.
I had no guard against the evil eye,
Though black men creep out of the water pail,
The picture book's Red Riding Hood
Has me in thrall for once and for all time.

Ether Stanzas

Pardon! I must jump off this ball;
in Paris a beautiful festival reigns.
Crowds collect in the Gare de l'Est
where bright silk banners wave as well.
You won't find me among them, though.
I've run off to this vast big room.
I mix myself in every dream,
a thousand looks and each I know.
A sick man lies in misery.
His last look hypnotizes me.
We long to go back to some lost summer day.
A black cross fills the room.

After the Cabaret

I see the early morning sun.
At five a.m. I homeward stroll.
The lights still burn in my hotel.
The cabaret is finally done.
In shadows children hunker down.
The farmers bring their goods to town.
You go to church, silent and old
grave sound of church-bells in the air,
and then a girl with untamed hair
wanders up all blear and cold:
"Love me, free of every sin.
Look, I've kept watch many nights ."

Dancer

To you it's like I'm marked, my name
just one on the list of the dead.
Too gone to sin in many ways,
I slowly drag through life's old game,
anxiety in every stride.
My very heartbeat's sick,
and it grows weaker day by day.
The angel of death now stands inside.
I dance until I'm out of breath –
I'll soon be in my grave –
I know I'll have no lover then –
so kiss me until death.

Two

Richard Huelsenbeck

Dada staked out very nearly the entire territory that has since been occupied by the avant-garde: multi-media, abstraction, bricolage, performance and conceptual art, found objects, use of tribal and popular culture, the cultivation of a privileged "hip" vision. Despite their seminal influence, though, actual dada works are often known only vaguely at second-hand. I have found in recent live performances of my translations that dada poetry can still bring an audience to attention. Even after nearly a century, competing with all the current varieties of spoken word, the works of Richard Huelsenbeck, Hans Arp , Hugo Ball, Emmy Jennings, and their colleagues remain scintillating with rebellion and spectacular in the eruption of unlikely images, but also ambitious far beyond their immediate shock value.

The title of Richard Huelsenbeck's autobiography *Memoirs of a Dada Drummer* defines his role both literally and figuratively. Huelsenbeck was a principal performer in the Cabaret Voltaire in Zurich. In Germany he participated in the provocations of the extravagant Oberdada Johannes Baader. Condemning the church and the Weimar regime, they demanded a Instead, insert after "they demanded" an extraordinary brand of radical communism. They thus maintained an altogether righteous anti-fascist, ant-capitalist passion at the same time as an apparently nihilistic vision.

Known for his insistence even during the 20s that "Germany must be defeated," he was to the Nazis a clear example of the "degenerate" artist and an obvious target. After emigrating to the USA (with the aid of Albert Einstein), he transformed himself into a Jungian analyst, later practicing "existential psychiatry"in Manhattan using the name Charles R. Hulbeck.

Huelsenbeck's poems are declamatory in their rhetoric and pyrotechnic in the speed and flash of their images, but they also have a kind of propulsive passion sometimes lacking in avant-garde works. The following poems are from his *Phantastische Gebete* [Fantastic Prayers] which was published first in 1916 and reissued in an expanded version with wonderful drawings by

George Grosz in 1920. In his 1959 preface to a new edition Huelsenbeck describes religion in terms that apply in fact to other symbolic manipulation such as visual art and particularly to his "prayers": "It is the experience of constructive will in the world which lends wings to the course of the stars despite all the fallen angels and helps man in the course of his life to understand the archetypal symbols of his existence." I believe these poems do no less.

Mafarka

Ravens circle lemon yellow
deepdark cold shadow-walls
of the shadow-walls has masks
o o ho oho in legs carved of wood
association and Baudelaire Mafarka blooms
the cherry tree blooms a blue clock-strike

slowly it rises from the dark it falls from the white against him faster it closes and violates perspective loosens itself posthaste in the vast surfaces teaches to worship cries the yellow the red o that Indian's red of the totem cries the death knell for the condemned the umbrellas call out rose madder slide swim over the fountains sitting and seating and seating and laughing and seating and laughing the quee-ee-een of porcelain the quee-ee-een the dragons toss their tongues over the capitals – o – o – o – the capitals are on fire the blue flames of the capitals strike across the seas so colorful together the seas amid the sound of flames o – o – the lassos whiz far off to the equator

Death

For Li

Death is greater than a porterhouse
he goes with monster eyes like two clouds of cinnabar
    through the land
so that the sun goes down in fainting fear the cop
    stands amazed
and the sea cries a great wonder! from his sleep
yes the hearse's procession with well-nourished corpses
    jostles carts
also virgins whose kisses froze on their lips and
    countenances
mother's body in fits god made the measureless
o he sings more powerfully than the priest's litany
    and steam rises and trumpets call
peoples disperse little crybabies o the helpless beg
god god god   he ties his coat round his haunches
breath comes in the cities where weeping on beds,
brokenhearted,
we have no choice but to wrap our minds about
the inconceivable
he's on our shoulders and necks before we suspect
anything

caresses tender cheeks and mouth dog
all-powerful killer revolutionary
we are attention and we are disregard as well
in that we're made in your image

End of the World

Indeed things have come to such a pass in this world
that cows sit atop the telegraph poles and play chess
the cockatoo sings so sad under the Spanish dancer's
skirts like a trumpeter from HQ
and the cannons complain
the whole day long
it's the lilac landscape Mr. Mayer spoke of
when he lost his eye
only the firefighting squad can drive the nightmare
from the
salon
but their hoses are all cut
yeah yeah Sonya you think the celluloid puppet's a
changeling
and shout, "God save the king!"
All the Monist Club is meeting on the steamer
Meyerbeer
the helmsman alone can conceive a high C
I pull an anatomical atlas from my toes
and set to serious study
have you seen that fish who's loitered by the opera
in a morning coat these last two days and nights?

Oh, oh, you great devil – oh, oh bee-keeper, base
commander
wants a wow-wow-wow, wants a woe-woe-woe
who doesn't know
what Daddy Homer wrote
war and peace I hold in my robe but I've decided
that mine will be a cherry flip
no one knows today if tomorrow he'll have been
the rhythm's beat on the coffin-lid
if someone had only the balls to tear the feather-tail
from the streetcar it is high time
zoology professors gather in the fields of grass
they avert rainbows with upturned palms
the great guru places tomatoes on his brow
you fill again the castle and copse
the roebuck whizzes the horse leaps
(who wouldn't go crazy at that)

To Ludwig the Flirt

Your leg hangs over me like a crescent moon;
it's altogether clear: your breasts pant like beasts
under the best Belgian lace
hey, waiter, café au lait and the paper and a glass of water
at bottom you're like your sisters with the swaying bellies
who creep along the gutters, ears pricked
for the whistle of morality and the flesh-eating pimps
the cowboy whose pants you took (with his alligator wallet)
told me all I need to know about your soul.
hey you old pig you're fifty years old,
but the high schoolers dream of you nightly
they dream – you come sneaking with a supple
cane
heating them up behind with what their hearts desire
hey you dirty old men you manipulator of girls you gypsies and
hotel thieves
pray yes pray if you get a kick that way
or swill yourselves smashed till the houses rise their drains
break
let the firefighters thunder driving rivers from their sleep
old bums I approach a bottle under my arm crazy
ghost

and is it you once more oh precious swine has the surgeon
caught sight of your belly grappling iron all ready
torch and anaesthesia
dada dada no one lives but you, oh my tender beloved

The One Who Speaks

Dadadada – the lady who has matched her old greatness the impotence of the street-sweepers has become a scandal who can say I am since you be and he be-s dulce et decorum est pro patria mori or be always true and honest or someone's falling down hard or one step and you stand in just your shirt who dares it knight-man or his squire and it rolls and boils and bubbles and hisses Corcordia be thy name already the giraffes burrow their heads in the sand always still the calfskin thunders not what do you want from me in my youth a beauty chases the other and the arctic hare jumps from the sacrum o ah o the black women on the precipice rage along banging on drums some crawl others fly some burst some plod on for many a longish descent what do they want from me in my youth lightning fast the young apes come down from my hair the blue horses are grazing on the plains of my teeth the RHINOCEROS crouches in first one breast than the other hum hum chop chop chop hum hum chop chop chop who brought the panther into the streetcar who kicks auntie in her rubber rear end I be o ladies and gents I am the experience since sunrise Mafarka the Futurist gave me three children and already the third stews in a casserole of shiny stainless steel for what did papa Homer say hit her chop her beat her till absinthe dances in her capillary tubes I am the Pope and the promise and the Liverpool latrine

DADA-Schalmei

on the flute big and simple
the Dadaist plays again
since on the stream the cricket chirps
and mo̊on makes love to night
tandaradei

o the soul is so dry
and the mind is confused
up where the clouds crouch
and terrible birds are wheeling
tandaradei

Yes, I play adagio
for the bride already dead
call it sadness, call it stupid o!
Man, you err as long as you keep eating!
tandaradei

to the spirit world she vanishes
as dawn draws near
she clings to giant glaciers

like a rhyme of old man Goethe
tandaradei

I give you the best,
a dada song, like a little fly
its wings lift it slowly in suspense
tandaradei
think of Tzara think of Arp
think, too, of the great Huelsenbeck
R. HUEL / SEN / BAG.

Streams

From spotty tubes spout streams in the shadows
of living trees
parrots and carrion vultures are always tumbling
from the twigs to the ground
futons are the walls of heaven and from the clouds
come parachuting magicians
towers have tied on cloudskin masks before their
bedazzled eyes
o you streams under the ponte dei sospiri you
collect lungs and livers and severed necks
but in the Hudson Bay a siren flew or a bird griffin or
a little housewife of the most
modern sort
with your hands you reach in the pockets of
bureaucrats stuffed with pensions all sorts of good
will and the best of liverwurst
what have we all done before your eyes how have we
all prayed
from the scorpion sting the holy singers' seats are
swollen
and Ben Akba the high priest is rolling in the shit

your veins are blue red green and orange colored like
    the faces of
ancestors in their Sunday best perching on top of altars
giant high hats of tin and brass make a heavenly concert
the forms of angels are suspended on the way out
    as the reflection of poisoned blooms
so you form your limbs over the horizon in waterfalls
from its sofabed the Indian Ocean arose with its
    ears stuffed with cotton
from your huts creep the hot waters and howl
they've pitched tents from morning till night over
    your lust and hordes of phonographs
  await the quacking of your lascivious desire
bad luck has come in the world.
the giant woman's breasts flame up and the
    snakeman gave birth to a rattail
Umba Umba the black tumbles from chicken coops
    and the froth of your breath touches
  your toes
a huge slaughter passed over you and over the
    sleep of your lips
a great murder fulfills you.

Tree

Slowly the house heap opened up the middle of its
    belly then
the swollen necks of churches howl to the depths
above
here they hunted like dogs the colors of all clay yet seen
all sounds ever heard hurtled rattling to the center
the colors and the sounds shattered like glass and
    cement and soft dark drops fell heavily
  down
the stars rattle in chorus now and hold a plate
    high in their hand
O Allah Cadabaudahojojo o hojohojolodomodoho
O Burrubu hihi o Burrubu hihi o hojolodomodoho
and white and strong old man ho
and mud-tossed kiosks ho
and those hours that are filled with the shimmer
    of bass trumpets
bassoons far gone in drink wandered to the pointy
    grille work and
casks in red suits junk welled up ho
oho oho o mezza notte that gave birth in the tree
the shadow whips beat your body now

the blood you dine on over the horizon is white
boats hung with banners fare forth between your
  breathing in and breathing out
oho oho over the mirror of your body the howl of
  the century flies
in your hair sit polished storms like parrots
in the wrinkles of your brow are crepe paper and tinsel
all kinds of butchery lies buried before you oho
see millions of gravestones are your midday meal
your clothes have that cadence of ebb and flow
and when you sing streams dance before you
oho joho
then you sing then your voice goes on
O Allah Cadabaudahojoho O hojohojolodomodoho
O Burrubuh hibi o burrubuh hihi a
  hojohojolodomodoho

Schalaben—Schalabei — Schalamezomai

Heads of horses drift on the blue flatlands
like great dark purple flowers
the moon's bright disc is surrounded by shrieks
of comets stars and glacierpuppets
schalaben schalabai schalamezomai
Canaanites and janizaries fight a great
fight on the bank of the red sea
heaven pulls in the flags heaven re-
places glass roofs over the fight of bright
arms
O you bright shadows of therebinth and pipeplant
o you joyous worshippers of the great god
behind veils horses sing a song of praise
to the great god
schalaben schalabai schalamezomai
the ear of the great god hangs over the combatants
like a shell made of glass
the cries of comets areheard from the shell
made of glass over countries over the fight over the
endless wars

the hand of god is as fine as the hand
of my lover
schalaben schalaben schalamezomai
the grass dries up in the general's body
he sees sitting on high chairs the shadows of the
midnight
sun
and the whiteness of the nearby sea and the harsh sound
of Vulcan's storms breaks out
and that's how god opens his mouth and caparison
fall and costly
bridles from the riding horse's back
and that's how god opens his mouth to burst the
fountains of the depths
which play over the hanged at the end of the world
though horses' heads hang on the comb of waves
schalaben schalaben schalamezomai
ai ai ai I saw a throne I sit in the chair of state
I saw ten times ten chairs of state and royal seats
I saw the beasts of the hoop of earth and I saw
metal birds
the heavens singing the endless praisesong of the lord
and the shining of phosphorus in heads obsessed schala
mezomai

and the swine stumbling to the sea called Lamana
strike on your breast that which can still flutter
out of gum
your tongue back over the horizon
wags with your ears so the ice cave shatters
I saw the bodies of the dead strewn over carpets
the dead fallen from church towers and the people
cried at the hour of judgment
I see the dead riding bass trumpets
on the day of the moon
red red are the heads of the horses that drift
on blue flatlands.

Three

Hans Arp

Child of an Alsatian mother and a German father, Hans Arp was born in Strassburg at a time when it was German. When it became French again at the end of WWI, French law mandated that he call himself Jean. Thus his very name draws attention to the nationalist contention that struck him as absurd.

An originator of the *Moderner Bund* ("Modern League") and an exhibiter with the *Blaue Reiter* group prior to being a founding member of the dada group in 1916 Zürich. The creator of sublime abstract sculpture and other visual work, Arp is also a major poet. Educated as an artist in both France and Germany, he was already dodging the draft in Switzerland when he was called up. He recounts writing the date in the first blank of a stack of forms, then proceeding to write the date in every other space, after which he painstakingly added the column of numbers thus produced. He then took off all his clothes, folded them with care, placed the paperwork on top and presented the stack to the officer in charge, upon which he was told he was unsuitable for the military.

Later associated with the highly political Cologne dada group, he also participated in the first Surrealist show at the Galerie Pierre in Paris. During the 'thirties he worked with the Paris-based group *Abstraction-Création* whose members, including Mondrian, Kandinsky, and Mary Cassatt, considered Breton's Surrealism to be dogmatic.

Arp pioneered abstract art, though his early association with Kandinsky is evident in his preference for van Doesburg's term "concrete" as more appropriate for forms that originate in the mind and occupy space. Regarding "the law of chance as the highest and deepest of laws," he employed aleatory elements in works such as his randomly tossed *papiers déchirés*. He loved to reshuffle image sets (as here in "Roses Stroll the Streets of Porcelain" and "Westoily Roses").

His poetry strikes me as a pyrotechnic display of images, a one-man band, a word-collage. He shares with a prominent school of poets today the proposition that, as Jacques Riviére said of the dadaists in general, for them language "is no longer a means; it is an entity." If his lyric persona is sometimes difficult to follow, this is hardly surprising given his goal of "break[ing] down the language into atoms, in order to approach the creative." In Arp the background is a vast and cosmic laugh and he does not shrink from whimsy, yet he insisted to the end that dada was no farce. Using the same religious language favored by Huelsenbeck, he notes of his circle of young revolutionaries "our lot of earthly joy was meager. But by way of recompense we were visited by angels".

Opus Null

1.

I am the great great Thisthatthey
a rig or ous re gime
the stem of ozone prima qua
the nameless one-percenter
The P. P. Tit and trom as well
trombone without a mouth or hole
I'm Hercules' great earthen bowl
the left foot of the right right chef.

I am the entire lifetime long
the ovary's dozeneth meaning
totality of Augustine
in cellulose gown preening

2.

He pulls from out his coffin black
one coffin, then another
he wraps himself in a black crepe sack
and weeps with his front end.
Half wizard and half maestro
without a cane the time he'll beat

a greeny clockface on his hat
and falls down from the driver's seat.

With that he pokes the ghetto fish
off his well-equipped easel. He
finds his long cubistic socks are torn
twice in two and thrice in three.

3.

He sits with himself in an arc.
A circle sits right by his side.
A bag that holds a comb that stands
must be his sofa and his bride.
The of-of and his left-hand skin
his own bag and his own life
and tick and tack and tipp and top
he own body falls from the wife.

4.

His steam dynamo turns out
hat upon hat from his hat and then
he stands them in formation in
a ring just as one does with army men.
He greets them then and tips his hat

and three times greets them all as friends
They always trust a caca-you
replaced by him with caca-too.

He sees them not but greets them still.
He's with them and they're all about.
The hats are all included
they screw the top from his ego.

WILLIAM SEATON

Roses Stroll the Streets of Porcelain

1

just on the edge of the fairy-tale
          the night knits roses for itself;
the tangle of things resolves into
          storks, fruits, pharoahs, and harps.
death puts down its nattering wreath
          by the root of the void.
and the storks chatter on chimneystones!
and the night is a stuffed fairy tale.

2

and the roses stroll the streets of porcelain and
knit from the tangle of their years
  one star after another.
between stars there sleeps a piece of fruit.
the empty lands stuffed years laughing foot-
lockers dance!
the storks eat the pharaohs.
from chimneystones roseblossoms!

3

death eats one year after another.
and pharaohs eat storks.
between fruits sleeps a star. often it laughs lightly
in its sleep
  like a porcelain harp.

4

growing chimneystones eat harps porcelain
wreaths dance.
pharoahs have roots of roses!
the storks pack chimneystones in their footlockers
and fly off
  to the land of the pharoahs!

WILLIAM SEATON

The Swallow Testicle

Oh no, oh no, good Kaspar's dead!
Who now will hide the burning banners in cloudbraid
  and daily build a black mare's nest?
Who now will turn the coffee mill in its old, old barrel?
And who will lure the idyllic deer
  from its petrified paper bag?
Who'll blow the noses of ships, parapluies, wind-udders, ancestral bees, ozone spindles,
  and who will bone the pyramids?
Oh no, no, no, our good Kaspar is dead! Pious bimbam Kaspar's dead!
The shark will rattle his teeth with heartrending grief when he hears his given name — so
  I sigh on — his last name Kaspar Kaspar Kaspar.
Why hast thou forsaken us? In what form has your great and beautiful soul
  transmogrified? Are you a star? or a chain of water hanging from a hot whirlwind? or
  a transparent brick on the groaning drum of rocky BEING?

Now our tops and toes dry up, and fairies lie half-charred on the funeral pyre.
Now the black bowling alley thunders behind the sun, and no one winds up compasses
and pushcart wheels any longer.
Who now will eat with the phosphorescent rat at the lonely barefoot table?
Who now will chase the siroccoco devil when he wants to fuck the horses?
Now who'll explain the monograms in the stars?

His bust will grace the mantel of all the truly noble men,
but that's no comfort, no tobacco snuff for a deadhead skull.

Second Ha-

that I as I
one and two is
that I as I
three and four is
that I as I
what time now
that I as I
it ticks, it tocks
that I as I
five and six is
that I as I
seven eight is
that I as I
if it stands it
that I as I
if it works then
that I as I
nine and ten is
that I as I
eleven and twelve is.

Baobab

And she was delivered of a healthy strong boy
who enjoyed the name Baobab.
The boy grew and grew
and grew up to the blue of heaven.
And Baobab's people liked to look
right in the eyes of interlocutors.
However, for one as tall as Baobab
this no longer could be done.
So they dug out lots of soil
and opened a great abysmal hole
in which Baobab entered by choice
for he too could never bear
not to look into the eyes
of those to whom he spoke.
The earth that they had dug
they tossed over their starlet's edge
into the bottomless space.
And after Baobab had had passed
a hundred years in this hole
he began to dwindle.
Every day he was smaller and smaller
until in the end he evanesced.

Westoily Roses

1

the roses will be crucified on hats the lips
the roses fly forth
the bloody organs drip on the visible
throne of the half-grown Near Eastern stones and
on the white skulls
the three shaven summers and the three shaven
crosses stagger forward on crutches like the May
the lyre body tells of bloody slaughter
against the hairy stones, the lyre body shoots out
a poison foam
stony crutches bloody noses hairy stones against
the shavehead skulls

2

the lyre body drips blood on the white shirtfronts
as though in a battle unpacked and tosses its
three snowballs behind its three summers
from the retorts roll the skulls of the Itosis
the lips of the hats return on crutches
gloves will be crucified on hats.

the crosses support one another half-human-like
by the bridegroom and the other half-mannish by
the bridegroom

3

the lyre body tells of the birth from foam of a
half-grown Near Eastern stone most certainly and
heath-soul sits on a visible throne and
tosses the bloodier parts of the foolhardy and
carthardy
on the fifth of May. then the foam birth shoots
poisonous
accent-hens against the signature-organ of
the lyre body clings to the clapper by their balled-
up wings
and rings out and the winged words fly forth.
wings shave the hairy hearts
the air of the bit shakes and calls who goes there
and that's the way it goes up and then down like
in a letter

4

it rings out in the heart
the foam birth wraps white May air in a
snow-letter
the half-grown Near Eastern stone throws its
three gloves over its three hats and clings
to the roses
the lyre body shaved the slaughter-clapper
winged roses fly to the snow-lyre.

Four

Hugo Ball

In Munich Ball was associated with Wedekind in the court theatre, the *Kammerspiele*. An actor who actually enlisted when the First World War began, Ball was in the army when German invaded Belgium, upon which he concluded that "the war is founded on a glaring mistake, men have been confused with machines." He deserted, emigrated to Switzerland, and pursued art and anarchism, translating Bakunin.

A few years later, however, he followed a spiritual tendency, perhaps similar at root to that animating Arp and Huelsenbeck, but which, for him, resulted to orthodox Catholicism and a pious and quiet lifestyle.

Ball was a major practitioner of the sound poem. In the Dada Manifesto of 1916, he says "I let the vowels quite simply occur, as a cat meows," and that document itself several times leaves off attacking the philistines to lapse toward abstract sound. His most celebrated work of this sort "gadji beri bimba," was performed by The Talking Heads on a 1979 album.

Ball's other work includes a biography of his friend Hermann Hesse, a novel titled *Flametti* or *The Dandyism of the Poor*, and a number of plays, including *Michelangelo's Nose*.

Caravan

jolifanto bambla o falli bambla
großiga m'pfa habla horem
egiga goramen
higo bloiko russula huju
hollaka hollala
anlogo bung
blago bung blago bung
bosso fataka
ü üü ü
schampa wulla wussa olobo
hej tatta gorem
eschige zunbada
wulubu ssubudu uluwu ssubudu
tumba ba-umf
kusa gauma
ba - umf

WILLIAM SEATON

The Dance of Death

to the tune of "That's how we live"

That's how we die, that's how we die,
We die every day.
Because it is so comfy to let go.
Mornings still in sleep and dream,
noontime already there,
by evening at the bottom of a grave.

Slaughter is our house of joy.
Blood is our only sun.
Death is our sign, our magic word.
We leave both wife and child,
What have they to do with us?
If one relies
on us alone . . .

So we murder, so we kill.
We murder every day
our comrades in a dance of death.
Brother, figure it out with me –
brother, your breast,

brother you must fall and die.
We don't murmur, we don't growl,
We're quiet every day
until the joint of the hip-bone turns.
Our camping ground is hard.
Our bread is dry.
Bloody and soiled our dear god.

We thank you, we thank you,
dear Kaiser, for your grace
in deciding to lie down and die.
Just sleep, sleep soft and still
Until you waken our poor body,
now covered by the lawn.

Afterword

Lament for the Loss of the Avant-Garde

I grew up committed to the avant-garde. Even beyond partisanship, the concept lay at the basis of my structuring of the world. One pole of every opposition was for me animated with life and energy while the other bore the dead weight of reaction: not only art and politics and religion split into camps of the hip and square, old and young, academic and revolutionary – the principle seemed at the time universal. Remember Norman Mailer's *Village Voice* lists from the 'fifties? Bohr's model of the atom is square, Heisenberg's hip, etc. (Though, of course, the line into the future could involve such radical exhumation of the past as pre-Raphaelitism and Pound's resurrection of the troubadours.)

This whole bipolar opposition is primarily a Romantic myth. In spite of boasts from millennia of artists and writers that they are "making it new," and in spite of the line of off-beat artists extending back to archaic schizoid shamans, and the ancient world's wine-drinker poets (in contrast to the soberly craftsmanlike water-drinkers), the idea of bohemia is, like the term, less than two hundred years old. But is course seems already to be run, thouh practitioners continue to go through the motions that used to *épater the bourgeoisie* though now these are the very gestures by which they court the embrace of the same bourgeoisie.

Now it is clear from oral and popular genres that art that defends the status quo may be great. Apart from exotic examples like African sculpture and oral epic, the USA's greatest contributions to world culture may well be, as Gilbert Seldes ventured to suggest several generations ago, in genuinely popular genres: movies and jazz. But to read gestures accurately, it is necessary to distinguish the glad hand from the cocked snoot.

In my opinion the last great era of the avant-garde was launched buy the dadaists in the early part of the past century and ripened in the great surrealist ventures of the next few decades. Admittedly, even here it was possible for a perversely conservative entrepreneur like Dali to evolve, but surely

Franco and the Pope always knew he was a character to keep at arm's length even if the buyers of his millions of limited editions did not.

The performances at the Café Voltaire genuinely amazed the public and went near the limit in cracking art's possibilities. No second appearance of Picabia in a tutu could replicate the first. Beyond sound poetry, what? Not only did these artists do things never dared before in the realm of taste and semiotic manipulation; they were altogether serious in their fierce opposition to those who held economic power. Whether communist like Breton and Huelsenbeck or anarchist like Bunuel, they struggled with the ruling class for control of art.

Now the Rockefeller Foundation is pleased to fund work that resembles nothing so much as the performance of the Duke and the Dauphin in *Huckleberry Finn*; the largest museums compete in bidding for the new; we find that the CIA promoted abstract expressionism as part of the cold war, and the once-radical designs of the Bauhaus embody the glittery apparition of American wealth in lower Manhattan. Andy Warhol, who seriously took up the task of representing the icons of our culture, not just soup cans and celebrities, but crack-ups as well, began in corporate advertising and spawned the *Interview* sensibility which fawns on the rich and particularly favors those who are vicious as well (the Marcoses, the Shah). Mapplethorpe, too, for all the fuss displays flawlessly elegant academic/advertising skills and is attacked only by know-nothings, with everyone in the art world from establishment to young lions defending his work.

Even real *art brut* styles have been easily digested from Rouault to Red Grooms, and what passed a few generations ago for derangement of the senses now sells jeans and cologne on MTV. Conceptual art may have been the last theoretical gasp of the avant-garde, for once everything is assimilated to art, what boundary remains to be challenged? What is the next move?

I offer no prescriptions for the resuscitation of the avant-garde. Some alternatives are clear: among the more common already current are antiquarianism, deeper probing of sore psychic regions, the sleazier sorts of pop culture, and borrowing from the tribal. I lament the passing of the avant-garde, and suggest we be conscious of its implications. What changes in society, in art, and in their relation have rendered obsolete the idea of an avant-garde, so seminal these past few centuries? Surely among the assassins of the avant-garde are the continuing marginalization of art, the greedy commodification of art processes, and the collapse of radical challenge in non-artistic realms. Under these conditions an active avant-garde would be a zombie-like walking corpse.

Nirala Series

A Series of Contemporary Writing

TEN: The New Indian Poets
Selected and Edited by
Jayanta Mahapatra & Yuyutsu Sharma
ISBN-81-8250-025-7 2012 pp.134 Hard

Milarepa's Bones, Helambu
33 New Poems
Yuyutsu RD Sharma
ISBN-81-8250-032-X 2012 Hard pp.82

Garuda & Other Poems of Astral Plains
David B. Austell
ISBN-81-8250-038-9 2012 Hard pp.64

Inside Out, Upside Down, & Round and Round
Poems Selected & New
John J. Trause
ISBN-81-8250-049-4 2012 Paper pp.83

All the way from Kathmandu
Selected Jazz Poems
John Clarke
ISBN-81-8250-042-7 2012 Paper pp.82

No Child More Perfect & Other Poems
Christi Shannon Kline
ISBN-81-8250-039-7 2012 Paper pp.8

Things Missed in Exile
New Poems
E. Avi Frishman
ISBN-81-8250-029-X 2012 Paper pp. 49

Journey Though India and Nepal : Poems/Pictures
Robert Scotto & Lu Wu
ISBN-81-8250-045-1 2012 Hard pp.82
Incident on the Orient
Poems by **George Wallace**
ISBN-81-8250-044-3 2012 Paper pp.63

Little Creek *& Other Poems*
David Austell
ISBN 81-8250- 031-1 2011 Hard pp.200

Lizard Licking, Donegal *& Other Poems*
Diane Hamilton
ISBN - 81-81-8250-033-8 2011 Paper

Annapurna Poems
Poems New and Selected
Yuyutsu RD Sharma
ISBN 81-8250-013-5 2008 Hard pp.150

The Price of Heaven
Travel Stories from India and Nepal
Evald Flisar
Translated from Slovene by the Author & Alan